Animal Body Coverings

Why Do
Snails and Other
Animals Have
Shells?

Holly Beaumont

heinemann
raintree

To contact Capstone Global Library please call 800-747-4992, or visit our web site www.capstonepub.com

Edited by Clare Lewis and Kristen Mohn
Designed by Richard Parker
Picture research by Svetlana Zhurkin
Production by Victoria Fitzgerald
Originated by Capstone Global Library

Library of Congress Cataloging-in-Publication Data
Beaumont, Holly, author.
  Why do snails and other animals have shells? / Holly Beaumont.
     pages cm.—(Animal body coverings)
  Includes bibliographical references and index.
  ISBN 978-1-4846-2536-1 (hb)—ISBN 978-1-4846-2541-5 (pb)—ISBN 978-1-4846-2551-4 (ebook) 1.
Body covering (Anatomy)—Juvenile literature. 2. Shells—Juvenile literature. 3. Animals—Adaptations—
Juvenile literature. 4. Adaptation (Biology)—Juvenile literature. I. Title.
  QL941.B43 2016
  591.47'7—dc23   2015000295

This book has been officially leveled by using the F&P Text Level Gradient™ Leveling System
Acknowledgments
The author and publisher are grateful to the following for permission to reproduce copyright material:
Joan Egert, 12, Kanjanee Chaisin, 20; Shutterstock: BlueOrange Studio, 16, Boyd Hendrikse, back cover
(right), 19, Goran Cakmazovic, 15, Igor Chervonenko, 17, Katie Smith Photography, 6, 22 (top left),
Kitsananan, cover (top), LauraD, 23 (algae), Lia Caldas, 13, 23, Maggy Meyer, 9, 23, Mike Bauer, 21, Pattara
Puttiwong, 8, pryzmat, 23 (hibernating snail), Reinhold Leitner, 4, 22 (bottom), 23, Sailorr, cover (bottom),
SnBence, back cover (left), 7, 22 (top right), Stacey Ann Alberts (tortoise shell), cover and throughout,
Vitalii Hulai, 5, Zoltan Major, 18; SuperStock: Biosphoto, 14, FLPA, 11, Juniors, 10

We would like to thank Michael Bright for his invaluable help in the preparation of this book.

Contents

Some words are shown in bold, **like this**. You can find them in the picture glossary on page 23.

Which Animals Have Shells?

Lots of different animals have shells. Many soft sea creatures have shells.

Snails have shells that sit on top of their bodies.

Shells are usually part of the animal's body. They usually grow as the animal grows.

This mussel's shells go all the way around it.

What Is a Shell?

A shell is a hard protective layer.

Most turtles and tortoises have bony shells.

Many sea creatures, such as this giant clam, have pairs of shells.

The shells have a hinge, like a door. They can open and shut.

What Are Shells For?

Shells keep the soft bodies of animals safe from **predators**.

Snails move slowly. They can't run away from birds. They carry their hiding place with them.

tortoise

This tortoise can pulls its legs and head inside its shell. It stays safely inside until the danger has gone.

How Do Shells Protect Snails in Winter?

Most snails don't like cold weather. They **hibernate** in the winter.

Snails seal the entrance of their shells with a thick mucus. This thick, slimy liquid dries hard.

dry mucus

The dry mucus and the shell help to keep the snail safe and warm.

Some snails hibernate in groups on tree trunks.

How Else Do Shells Help Animals?

Shells can protect snails from drying out. If the weather is too warm and dry, snails hide in their shells.

They poke their heads out when the weather is cooler and wetter.

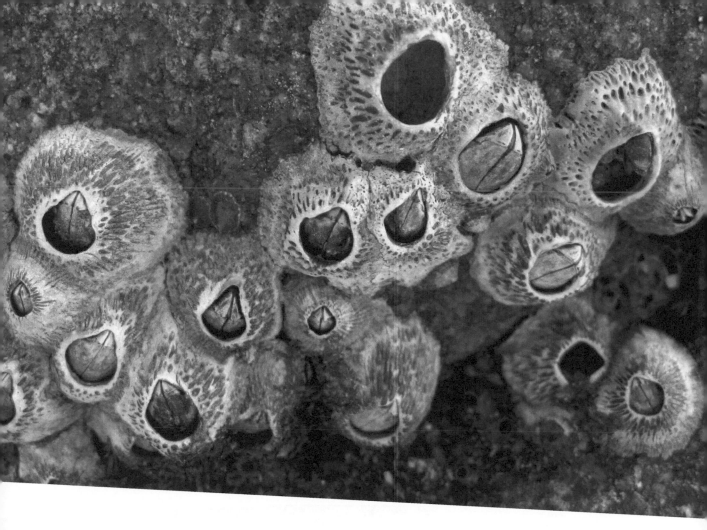

Barnacles are small animals that live in shells on underwater rocks.

When the tide is out, they close their shells tightly. This keeps them **moist** until the tide comes back in.

Are Snails Born with Shells?

When snails are born, they have small, soft shells. To make them stronger, they need **calcium**.

They get calcium by eating old shells and animal droppings. They even bite stones.

newest part

oldest part

As a snail gets older,
its shell grows in a spiral shape.

The oldest part is in the middle. The newest
part is on the outside.

How Do Other Shells Change?

Young turtles have very soft shells. Their shells cannot protect them from **predators**. They quickly run to the water after they hatch.

As turtles get older, their shells get harder.

Hermit crabs do not have shells of their own. They crawl into the seashells of other animals that have died.

As a hermit crab gets bigger, it finds bigger shells to live in.

How Do Animals Carry Their Shells?

Shells are useful, but they are also heavy.

Snails are very strong for their size. They can easily carry their shells.

This giant Galapagos tortoise has thick, strong legs. They help it to carry its huge shell around.

How Do Animals Take Care of Their Shells?

If a snail's shell gets damaged, the snail might dry out and die.

Small cracks usually heal by themselves.

crack on shell

Green turtles take care of their shells with the help of special fish.

Cleaner fish gobble up the **algae** that grow on turtle shells. This keeps the turtle shell clean and healthy.

Shells Quiz

Which of these images shows a snail shell?

A

B

C

Picture Glossary

algae   plant-like living thing

barnacle   small sea creature that lives in a shell and attaches itself to rocks on the beach

calcium   mineral you get from your food to help build your bones and teeth. Snails use it to help build their shells.

hibernate   to spend the winter sleeping or inactive

moist   slightly wet or damp

predator   animal that hunts and eats other animals

Find Out More

Web sites

Facthound offers a safe, fun way to find Internet sites related to this book. All of the sites on Facthound have been researched by our staff.

Here's all you do:

Visit *www.facthound.com*

Type in this code: 9781484625361

Books

Arthur, Alex. *Shell* (DK Eyewitness). New York: Dorling Kindersley, 2013.

Spilsbury, Louise. *Sea Turtle* (A Day in the Life: Sea Animals). Chicago: Heinemann Library, 2011.

Index